Experiments with
MATERIALS

T R E V O R   C O O K

W
FRANKLIN WATTS
LONDON • SYDNEY

First published in 2009 by Franklin Watts

Copyright © 2009 Arcturus Publishing Limited

Franklin Watts
338 Euston Road
London NW1 3BH

Franklin Watts Australia
Level 17/207 Kent Street, Sydney, NSW 2000

Produced by Arcturus Publishing Limited,
26/27 Bickels Yard, 151–153 Bermondsey Street,
London SE1 3HA

The right of Trevor Cook to be identified as the author
of this work has been asserted by him in accordance
with the Copyright, Designs and Patents Act 1988.

Editor: Alex Woolf
Designers: Sally Henry and Trevor Cook
Consultant: Keith Clayson
Picture Credits: Sally Henry and Trevor Cook

Every attempt has been made to clear copyright.
Should there be any inadvertent omission,
please apply to the publisher for rectification.

A CIP catalogue record for this book is available
from the British Library.

Dewey Decimal Classification Number: 620.1'1

ISBN 978 0 7496 8349 8

Printed in China

Franklin Watts is a division of Hachette Children's Books,
an Hachette Livre UK company.
www.hachettelivre.co.uk

Contents

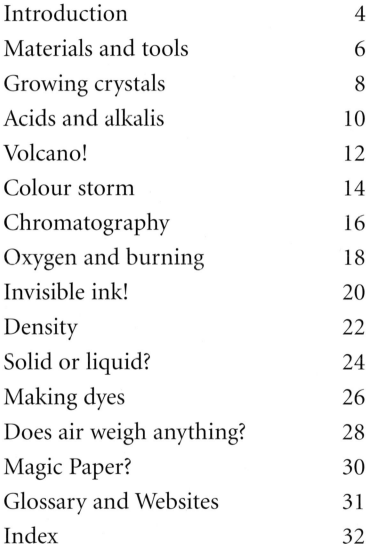

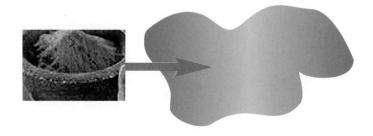

Introduction

Materials are all around and inside us. Our bodies are made up mostly of carbon, hydrogen, oxygen, nitrogen, calcium and phosphorus.

Carbon is the fourth most common element in the universe. It is also found in the form of diamonds, charcoal and pencil 'lead', as graphite.

This symbol is a corrosive chemical warning.

Hydrogen, a gas, is the most common element. With oxygen, it forms water as well as corrosive chemicals.

Oxygen is used in welding

Oxygen is the third most common element and makes up 21 per cent of air.

In May 1937, a famous German airship, the Hindenburg, burst into flames near its mooring mast in New Jersey, USA. Hydrogen and oxygen made an explosive mixture.

78 per cent of air is nitrogen. It's a gas that helps to make rocket fuel, explosives and fertiliser.

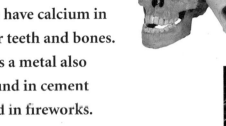

We have calcium in our teeth and bones. It is a metal also found in cement and in fireworks.

Phosphorus is a metal that self combusts when exposed to air.

It's used in making fertilisers and matches.

Some technical or unusual words, shown in *italic* type, are explained in the glossary on page 31.

Materials and tools

You should easily find many things that you need for our experiments around the home.

 20 minutes

This tells you about how long a project could take.

 This symbol means you might need adult help.

Jam jars Try to save as many different clean, empty jars at home as you can. We are going to need quite a few for the experiments. Afterwards you can recycle them.

Ice lolly sticks These are ideal for stirring mixtures or lighting night lights. Collect them next time you eat ice lollies!

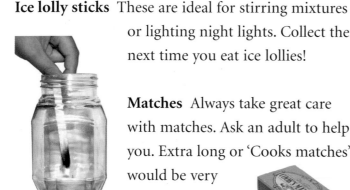

Matches Always take great care with matches. Ask an adult to help you. Extra long or 'Cooks matches' would be very useful in some of our experiments.

Night light Just like small candles, but with a metal case, night lights are safer and more stable than candles. Be sure to handle with care. Never leave lighted candles or night lights unattended.

Kitchen supplies Be careful when using food ingredients or anything from unmarked bottles. Check with an adult and get permission first.

Mixing bowl This will be essential for several projects. Use a plastic bowl if you can.

Kettle You will sometimes need to use boiling water. Ask an adult to help. Check that the kettle is turned off when you have finished with it.

Tongs Very useful for gripping hot things.

Plastic dropper Available from art and craft shops, ideal for controlling drops of liquid.

Scissors Use safe scissors that you can keep for all your science experiments. Keep them away from young children.

Funnel Very useful for filtering liquids when used with filter paper or kitchen roll. Also handy for filling bottles.

Baking tray A metal tray, normally used in the oven, will be very useful to you for the 'Volcano' project, as it could get a bit messy!

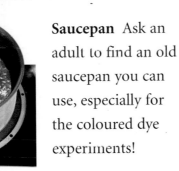

Saucepan Ask an adult to find an old saucepan you can use, especially for the coloured dye experiments!

String Ordinary household string will be fine for most of our needs.

Balloons Next time you have a party, keep a few balloons for use in our balancing experiment! (see page 28)

Notebook
Keep a special notebook to record the results of your experiments.

Coloured markers
You will find it handy to have a box of water-soluble coloured pens for several of the projects. For 'Chromatography' on page 15, you will need to use at least six different colours.

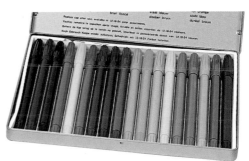

Friends can help
Do the experiments with your friends when you can, especially when you can amaze them with magic! (see page 30)

Growing crystals

A crystal is a solid material which forms itself into a very regular three-dimensional pattern. Crystals are formed when a liquid cools and turns into a solid. The arrangement of *atoms* in the solid produces the shape of the crystal. An example of this is when water is cooled and becomes ice.

You will need:

- sugar, glass jar
- coarse string, an ice lolly stick
- hot water, spoon
- salt, sand, soil
- 2 jam jars, plastic bag
- coffee filter paper or kitchen towel
- funnel and a side plate

The plan

We are going to *dissolve* some substances in water. We will try to grow crystals. Then we will use crystallisation to purify salt.

Experiment 1

water level

end of string

1 Put some hot water into a jam jar. Water from the hot tap should be hot enough.

2 Add sugar, one spoon at a time, using the lolly stick as a stirrer. Keep adding more sugar until you can't dissolve any more. You will see undissolved sugar left at the bottom of the jar.

3 Tie the string to the lolly stick, hang it in the sugar solution and leave to cool. The string is a good surface for growing crystals.

4 As the solution cools, crystals begin to form on the string. Be patient, it can take a few days for crystals to form, provided you have made a saturated solution.

What's going on?

The sugar dissolves in water to form a sugar solution. Hot water allows more sugar to dissolve. As the water cools it cannot hold as much sugar in solution, and some sugar changes back to a solid.

What else can you do?

Try different kinds of sugar! Soft brown, golden castor, demerara – check in your kitchen cupboard.

Experiment 2

1 Mix salt, soil and sand together thoroughly with a spoon, on a piece of plastic bag.

2 Stir the mixture into warm water and leave to settle overnight.

3 Pour the liquid through a filter paper, taking care to leave the sediment in the bottom of the jar. Leave the filtered liquid on the plate in a warm place.

What's going on?

Only the salt dissolves in the water. Letting the solution stand allows the heavier particles of sand and soil to be pulled to the bottom of the jar by gravity. Filtering removes the smaller sand and soil particles. Finally, on the plate, the water *evaporates* to leave just the salt crystals.

Acids and alkalis

All liquids are either acids, neutral or *alkaline*. Examples of acids are acetic acid (in vinegar) and citric acid (in oranges and lemons). Strong acids can eat away metal. Very strong *alkalis* can cause chemical burns.

You will need:
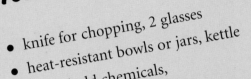

- knife for chopping, 2 glasses
- heat-resistant bowls or jars, kettle
- household chemicals,
- plastic dropper
- red cabbage

The plan

We are going to make an *indicator* that will tell us which liquids are acidic and which are alkaline.

What to do:

1 Ask an adult to chop about two cupfuls of cabbage into small pieces. Place them in the bowl.

2 Pour some boiling water onto the red cabbage and leave for 15 minutes. Ask an adult to pour the kettle.

3 Pour off the liquid into a bowl. This liquid is our 'indicator'.

4 You need two known liquids to test your indicator. We are using white vinegar (acid) and a solution of bicarbonate of soda in water (alkali).

5 Add indicator to your solution in drops. Watch the indicator colour change. Wash the glasses thoroughly between tests.

6 See where the results fall on this chart.

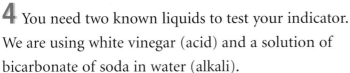

◄ more acidic		neutral		more alkaline ►
red	purple	blue-violet	blue-green	green-yellow

What else can you do?

Try other kinds of coloured vegetable juice to see if they make indicators.

What's going on?

The *pigments* from the cabbage react with acids and alkalis to change the colour. The juice should turn pink in acidic solutions and green in alkaline ones.

Put some indicator drops in plain water. This is your neutral colour. Use your indicator to test other liquids and compare the results.

Jargon Buster
Acids are found in citrus fruits.
Alkalis are found in soap.

11

Volcano!

about 2 hours

We are going to take another look at acids and alkalis. The *volcano* is the effect we sometimes get when we mix the two! Get some friends to help!

The plan

We are going to show what happens when an acid is mixed with an alkali.

You will need:

- flour, salt, cooking oil
- tablespoon, 2 old baking trays
- large bowl, funnel, small plastic bottle
- red food colouring, mixing jug
- washing-up liquid, bicarbonate of soda
- warm water, vinegar
- black paint, paintbrush, *glitter*

What to do:

1 For salt dough, mix together 6 cups of flour, 2 cups of salt, 4 tablespoons of cooking oil and 1.5 cups of water in a large bowl. Work all the ingredients together until smooth and firm.

2 Stand the bottle on the baking tray. Mould the salt dough around the base of the bottle.

3 Build the dough up into a cone shape. Cover the bottle right up to the top, but don't let any dough fall in. When dry, roughly paint the cone black. Add some glitter.

4 Mix 10 drops of red food colouring with warm water. Pour 400ml (half a pint) into the bottle.

5 Put 8 drops of washing-up liquid into the bottle.

6 Add 3 tablespoons of bicarbonate of soda, to create 'lava'.

7 Pour in vinegar to fill the bottle, and remove the funnel. Stand well back!

8 Watch the foaming 'lava' as it pours down the volcano! Take care not to get any food colour on your clothes!

What's going on?

The vinegar is an acid. The bicarbonate of soda is an alkali. They react together violently producing (amongst other things) carbon dioxide gas. As gases take up more space than solids and liquids, the mixture bubbles up and out of the bottle.

Warning!

Do not try mixing other household chemicals unless you are sure it is safe to do so! Ask an adult.

What else can you do?

Try putting the red cabbage indicator from page 10 into white vinegar and then add bicarbonate of soda, a little at a time. What do you think will happen to the indicator?

Jargon Buster
Lava is molten rock which erupts from a volcano – as hot as 1200 °C!

Colour storm

45 minutes

Oil and water don't mix. Or do they? Here we show in a very colourful way the difference a little washing-up liquid can make.

You will need:

- 2 white plates or saucers
- full fat milk
- washing-up liquid
- matchstick or skewer
- 3 or 4 colours of food colouring
- notebook and pencil

The plan

We are going to add food colouring to water and then to milk. Then we'll see what happens when we drop washing-up liquid into the mixtures.

1 Pour water into a saucer or plate. Wait for a minute or until the water stops moving.

2 Put some evenly spaced drops of food colouring in the water.

3 Pour some milk into the other saucer or plate. Wait for a minute for the milk to stop moving.

4 Put some drops of food colouring in the milk, evenly spaced.

5 Add one drop of washing-up liquid to each of the saucers.

6 Look at your saucers after a few minutes, then again after 10 minutes.

7 Look at your saucers again after 20 minutes. Use a notepad and pencil to write down the results.

Make notes of what you see:

● What happens when you add the food colouring to the water?
● What happens when you add the colouring to the milk?
● What happens when you add the washing-up liquid to the water and milk?
● Read on to find out why.

What's going on?

Milk is a special mixture of fat and water called an emulsion. The fat is not dissolved in the water, but the two are mixed together. (If your milk has cream on the surface, that is because some of the fat has separated and floated to the top.)

The food colouring doesn't travel through milk as readily as it does through water because it mixes with only the watery part of the milk.

When you add washing-up liquid, two things happen – the surface tension of the water is *destroyed*, and the fat and water start to mix together because the washing-up liquid breaks up the fat.

The movement of the food colouring shows you what's happening. It moves to the side of the saucer when the surface tension is broken, and it swirls in patterns as the fat and water mix together.

What else can you do?

Try using a saucer of vegetable oil. What do you think will happen? Try other different liquids, or liquids at different temperatures.

Try not to spill the oil, as it can be hard to clean and it can stain things.

Jargon Buster
Food colouring is harmless, but it will stain your hands and clothes.

Chromatography

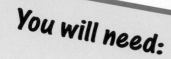

Chromatography is a technique for separating and identifying the parts that make up a mixture.

The plan

We are going to use one type of chromatography, called paper chromatography, to find out what pigments make up different coloured inks.

You will need:

- coloured felt-tip pens (not *permanent* or *waterproof*)
- blotting paper
- ruler, scissors
- tape, bowl, water
- pencil, notebook

What to do:

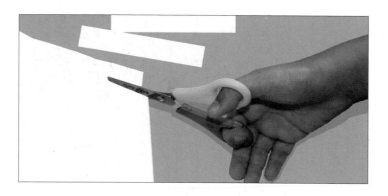

1 Cut blotting paper into strips, 100 x 15 mm (6 x 0.5 in).

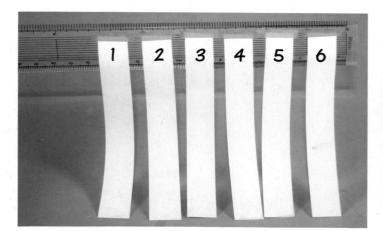

2 Number the strips and tape them to the ruler.

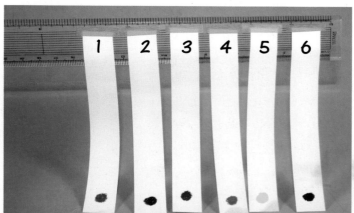

3 Put a small dot of different colour on each strip, noting each strip number as the colour is put on.

16

4 Fill the bowl half full with water. Hang the strips over the edge of the bowl, so that the ends are just touching the water.

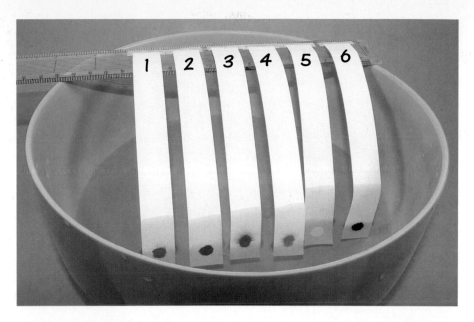

5 Wait until the water is 20 mm (0.75 in) or so from the ruler, then remove the strips from the bowl and record the colours you see. Sometimes a black will give a very surprising result!

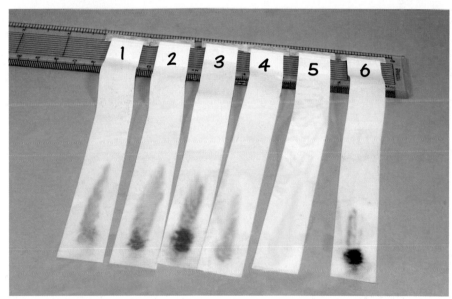

What's going on?

Water moves up the strips by capillary action and carries the pigments with it. Some pigments are more strongly attracted to the paper fibres and so are not carried so far. A colour may be made of many different pigments.

What else can you do?

Try using other coloured substances, for example food dye.

Jargon Buster
Capillary action is the way a liquid such as water is drawn into tiny spaces in a material by the attraction between molecules.

Oxygen and burning

35 minutes

One of the *components* of air is oxygen. Without it we would not be able to breathe and nothing would burn!

The plan

We are going to investigate what happens when a candle is burnt in a sealed jar.

Experiment 1

1 Put the candle in the base of the jar.

2 Put a few drops of water in the jar. Don't wet the wick!

3 Light the lolly stick with a match, then use it to light the night light.

4 When the night light is burning well, screw the lid down on the jar.

5 When the flame has gone out, use the indicator to test the water in the jar. It should prove acidic.

What's going on?

The candle needs oxygen to burn. With the lid closed, it uses up the oxygen in the jar. When there is none left, the flame goes out. Burning produces carbon dioxide (CO_2), some of which dissolves in the water to make carbonic acid.

18

Experiment 2

1 Use a clean jar. Place an empty cotton reel inside the jar, and put the night light on it to raise it up.

2 Carefully spoon three teaspoons of baking powder into the jar. Keep the powder off the night light.

3 Light a lolly stick with a match so you can reach the wick to light the night light. Or you could use a long match as we did.

4 Put about 10 teaspoons of vinegar into a jug and pour it very slowly onto the baking powder round the edges of the jar. Take care to avoid the night light.

5 Watch what happens! The powder turns to foam.

What's going on?

An *invisible* gas, carbon dioxide (CO_2), forms and puts the flame out! CO_2 is heavier than air, which it *displaces* in the jar.

Jargon Buster

Carbon dioxide (CO_2) is produced by all animals, plants, fungi and microorganisms when they breathe.

Invisible ink!

It's easy to send secret messages to your friends when you write them in top secret invisible ink. The 'secret' is in the combination of lemon juice and heat from a light bulb or an iron. The heat causes a chemical change in the lemon juice and makes it appear darker on paper.

The plan

It can be a little tricky to write with the 'ink' – it's invisible, after all – but once you get the hang of it, it's a fun way to share secrets with your friends. Let's try drawing a treasure map first!

You will need:

- toothpick
- lemon
- small knife
- paper
- side plate, small container
- heat source, such as a light bulb or iron

What to do:

1 Ask an adult to cut a lemon in half for you. Squeeze the lemon juice into a small bowl.

2 The lemon juice is your 'ink'! Dip the round end of a toothpick into the bowl.

20

3 Draw a secret map on some paper. Use lots of lemon juice for each part you draw.

4 Allow the paper to dry until you can't see the drawing any more!

5 Now move the paper back and forth under a heat source. As the ink gets warm, your secret map is revealed.

What's going on?

The acid in the lemon juice breaks down the *cellulose* of the paper into sugars. The heat supplied tends to *caramelise* the sugars, making them brown and revealing the secret drawing.

What else can you do?

Repeat this activity with vinegar or milk to find out which makes the best invisible ink.

Density

20 minutes

If we took similar sized cubes of wood and lead, the lead one would be much heavier. This is because lead is more dense than wood. It has more material packed into the same space.

You will need:

- jam jar, 3 drinking glasses
- various liquids and solids: syrup, cooking oil, water, grape, plastic wine cork
- blue and red food colouring
- plastic dropper, coin

The plan

We are going to compare the densities of different substances, then look at how temperature might affect density.

Experiment 1

cooking oil

water

syrup

1 Gently pour the cooking oil, syrup and water into a glass, one at a time.

2 Let the liquids settle. They should form distinct layers.

3 We are going to put the grape, the coin and the cork into the jar. Where do you think they will settle?

grape in water on top of syrup

cork floats in oil

coin sinks to base of syrup

What's going on? The various substances float or sink according to their densities.

Experiment 2 Using food colouring, follow stages 1–4.

1 Take a small glass of cold water and add some drops of blue food colouring. Put it in the fridge for an hour or so.

2 Take a small glass of hot water (from the tap) and add some red food colouring.

3 Half fill a tall glass with the blue water from the fridge.

4 Use the dropper to transfer small amounts of the red water into the blue water. The idea is not to mix the two colours. Keep the end of the plastic dropper near the surface.

What's going on?

If you've managed to do this experiment carefully enough, there should be two distinct layers. What do you think the position of the layers tells us about their density?

Warm water is less dense than cold water, therefore the red coloured water stays above the blue water in the glass.

Solid or liquid?

30 minutes

Materials can exist in three states – solid, liquid and gas. Some substances can have the *characteristics* of more than one state.

The plan
We are going to find out how difficult it is to tell a solid from a liquid!

You will need:

- 1 cup of cornflour
- half a cup of water
- bowl, mixing spoon
- food colouring (just for fun)

What to do:

1 Mix together the cornflour, the colouring and the water. It should become quite thick, but still feel like a liquid.

2 Try stirring the mixture quickly and then very slowly. What happens?

Jargon Buster
Cornflour can stand up to freezing or prolonged cooking!

3 Try to squeeze the mixture between your fingers. What happens?

4 Take some mixture in your hand and try to roll it into a ball.

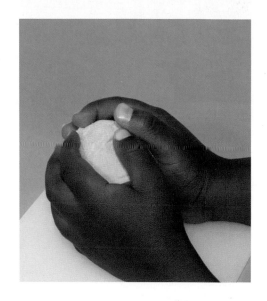

5 Put the ball down on a hard surface and hit it with your hand. (Be very careful with your hand!)

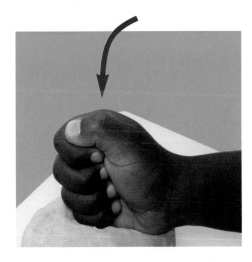

What's going on?

Cornflour and water form a *colloid* rather than a solution. This means that the particles of cornflour stay as a solid but are spread throughout the liquid. A colloid has unusual properties. You can stir it or let it run through your fingers like a liquid. When you try and move through it quickly (stirring fast) it resists. When you hit it, it shatters!

What else can you do?

Ketchup has colloid properties. What does this tell you about the best way to get it out of the bottle?

Jargon Buster
Colloid comes from the Greek word for glue.

Making dyes

You will need:

- an old saucepan, use of stove
- water, fork, tongs
- strips of white cotton material (from an old pillowcase or sheet would be ideal)
- plant material, such as onion skins, tea bags, turmeric, beetroot, acorns, walnuts, red cabbage, spinach, madder root (rubin), blackberries

The colours of objects around us are created by *pigments*. Some pigments are synthetic (man made) but many occur naturally.

The plan

We are going to make dyes from different plant materials.

What to do:

1 Take one of your collected materials. We chose blackberries. Wash and mash up with a fork.

2 Place the bits of plant in a saucepan with tap water. Put the saucepan on the stove.

3 Boil until the water is coloured. Ask an adult to help you use the stove.

4 Turn off the heat. Put a piece of white cloth into the saucepan.

5 When the cloth has taken on colour, just allow the saucepan to cool. Lift out the cloth using tongs.

6 Compare the dyed cloth with the original plant colour.

What's going on?

Crushing and boiling destroys the plant cells and releases the pigment. The pigment attaches itself to the cotton, which is absorbent.

What else can you do?

Try soaking or washing the cloth strips to see whether the colour stays. Try out your other plants. These are the sort of colours you might get:

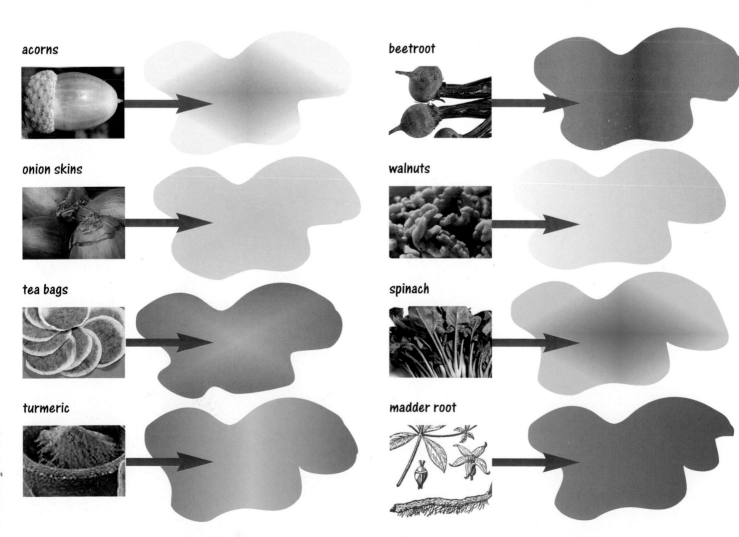

acorns

onion skins

tea bags

turmeric

beetroot

walnuts

spinach

madder root

Does air weigh anything?

30 minutes

You will need:

- 2 balloons
- string
- scissors
- thin piece of wood, about 600mm (2ft) long.
- balloons, marker pen

The plan

To find out if air weighs anything.

What to do:

1 Make marks about 10 mm (0.75 in) from each end of the piece of wood.

2 *Suspend* the wood by a piece of string, so that it hangs horizontally. This is our weighing *balance*.

 **Jargon Buster**
Air contains nitrogen, oxygen, argon, carbon dioxide and water vapour.

3 Cut two pieces of string the same length – about 150 mm (6 in). Make a loop at the end of each piece, just big enough to slip over the wood.

4 Take two similar balloons. Blow them both up, tie off the neck of one, but let the air out of the other.

5 Tie each balloon to one of the strings.

6 Slip the strings onto the stick, exactly on the 10 mm marks.

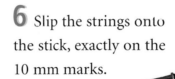

What's going on?

The only difference between the two balloons is that one is 'empty' and the other is full of air. But the air in the balloon is slightly compressed, so it is denser than the air around it, making the scale tip down.

What else can you do?

Try this puzzle! You'll need a kitchen scale and a glass of water. Place the glass of water on the scale: note the weight. Now, if you put your finger into the water without touching the glass, will the weight on the scale be more or less? Answer: see below.

Answer: More, because you add the volume of water displaced by your fingers to the weight.

29

Magic paper?

15 minutes

This amazing trick depends upon materials burning at different temperatures!

You will need:

- piece of paper (taken from a notebook)
- *methylated spirits*, salt, water
- night light, matches
- old saucer, metal tongs

The plan

You are going to astound your friends and family by setting fire to paper – without destroying it. This one needs an audience!

What to do:

1 Prepare a mixture of equal parts of methylated spirits and water. Add a pinch of salt.

2 Place the night light away from the solution before you light it.

1 metre (3.25 ft)

3 Soak the paper in the solution until it is thoroughly wet.

4 Pick up the paper with the tongs and drain off the excess liquid.

5 Move away from the solution, light the paper and watch it burn.

What's going on?

The methylated spirits burns at a relatively low temperature, which is not hot enough to evaporate the water. So the paper stays wet and doesn't burn. The salt makes the flame visible. Without it, the flame would be hard to see in daylight.

Glossary

Alkali *(noun)*   A substance that forms a chemical salt when combined with an acid.

Alkaline *(adjective)*   A compound that contains an alkali.

Atom   The smallest particle that makes up a chemical element.

Balance   A method used to compare weights of objects (see page 20).

Caramelise   Heat sugar or syrup until it has melted and turned brown.

Cellulose   Main part of plant cell walls and vegetable fibres.

Characteristic   Feature or quality of a particular person, place or thing.

Colloid   A gluey mixture of two substances which can behave like a liquid and a solid.

Components   Parts of something larger.

Destroy   Put an end to the existence of something by damaging or attacking it.

Displace   Take the place of something, to move away.

Dissolve   Become mixed into a liquid to form a solution.

Evaporate   Turn from liquid into vapour, to disappear.

Glitter   Decorative plastic fragments with mirrored surfaces which add sparkle to finishes.

Indicator   Used here to describe a liquid with known properties which reacts to acid or alkali.

Invisible   Unable to be seen.

Permanent   Of colours and paints: not water-soluble; hard to to remove.

Pigment   A material that changes the colour of light it reflects.

Neutral   In chemistry, a neutral solution is neither acidic nor alkaline.

Methylated spirits   A poisonous solvent, mainly ethyl alcohol (95 per cent) with added purple colouring.

Suspend   Hang something, normally from string or wires.

Volcano   An opening in the Earth's crust, which allows hot, molten rock, ash and gases to escape from below the surface.

Waterproof   Of colours and paints: not water-soluble, can't be washed out.

Water-soluble   Of colours and paints: can be washed out or dissolved with water.

Index

Websites

http://www.sciencekidsathome.com/
http://pbskids.org/zoom/activities/sci/
http://www.abc.net.au/spark/experiments/list.htm
http://kids.nationalgeographic.com/Activities/FunScience